D1633702

risk
management

helping directors to control
the risks that threaten you
and your business

sub-editor:	Lesley Malachowski
production manager:	Lisa Robertson
design:	Halo Design
client sales manager:	Fiona O'Mahony
commercial director, DP Ltd:	Ed Hicks
commercial director, IoD:	Sarah Ready
publishing director:	Tom Nash
chief operating officer:	Andrew Main Wilson

Published for the Institute of Directors and HSBC
Insurance Brokers by Director Publications Ltd
116 Pall Mall London SW1Y 5ED
Ⓣ 020 7766 8950 Ⓦ www.iod.com

© Copyright May 2006 Director Publications Ltd
A CIP record for this book is available from the British Library
Printed and bound in Great Britain.

HSBC Insurance Brokers

HSBC Insurance Brokers is one of the largest international insurance broking, risk management and employee benefits organisations in the world.

At HSBC Insurance Brokers we strive to provide our clients with the confidence and certainty to pursue their objectives. Since 1808, we have been providing informed advice and innovative solutions in many specialist areas of insurance, from Accident, Health and Contingency to Shipping Services. We deliver timely, effective and insightful service to all our clients through three specialist customer groupings:

direct client solutions

Joined up thinking for all the insurance and risk management requirements of Corporate and Commercial companies in the UK and worldwide. This grouping also includes our specialty areas: Education, Estates and Private Clients and Professional Indemnity.

international and intermediary solutions

Innovative thinking for specialist areas of Construction, Energy, Marine and Aviation, and Financial risks including Financial Institutions and Directors' and Officers' business. This area also controls our rapidly growing captive Management businesses in Bermuda, the Cayman Islands, the USA and Guernsey. Our Wholesale business area serves clients who are predominantly other intermediaries – areas such as cargo, our Intermediary Marketing Division and Specie.

reinsurance solutions

Leading-edge broking and consulting services to underwriters through the Reinsurance Treaty division, facultative business through the International Property and Casualty business area, and connected representative offices in Italy and Sweden.

CONTENTS

managing your business risks

**Miles Templeman, Director General
Institute of Directors**

In a world of increasing complexity and uncertainty, companies must manage risk more rigorously than ever. It is an essential aspect of good corporate governance today. Surprisingly, however, many still fail to do so, perhaps because they are overwhelmed by the size of the task or because they feel they lack the expertise to tackle it. Even more worrying, some remain blissfully unaware of the nature of the risks they face.

Thorough risk management strategies can enable businesses to identify possible threats – be they legal, financial, environmental or operational – and to introduce systematic plans for mitigation. Those companies that adopt this type of logical and structured approach to business risks are much more likely to survive and prosper.

The balance between risk and reward is the very essence of business: you have to take risks in order to generate returns and, generally speaking, higher returns involve greater risks. However, there is a difference between risks taken as a result of careful judgement and those taken unwittingly.

This Director's Guide will help companies develop a sound strategy for managing business risks, reducing their vulnerability to threats, both present and future. Such a strategy will also assist in the day-to-day management of the business, and help them to benefit from a reduction in costs and insurance premiums.

understanding your risk profile

Mike Dixon, Chief Executive
HSBC Insurance Brokers

Risk is present in every business activity that we undertake.

As directors, we accept that we run a risk when we launch a new product, or deliver a service. We understand that as business managers we have risks relating to cashflow, to profitability and to security.

When we grant credit to a client, we recognise the risk that the client may be unable to pay us for our goods and services. If we trade abroad we need to manage the risks of fluctuations in currency and potential political disturbance in those areas with which we trade.

We are exposed to risks that relate to the employment of people – who may make mistakes – and to the risks surrounding our use of computer systems – that may fail. We confront daily the possibility that our processes may be flawed or that external catastrophic events may impact upon the success of our business.

We can only avoid risk in business by ceasing to trade, and so, if we are to be successful in business we must manage risk. As directors, we are responsible for deciding which risks are appropriate for our business, and which should be transferred or avoided.

To fulfil this responsibility successfully, we need to understand the risks we run, to evaluate the likelihood of those risks turning to reality, and to recognise the potential impact if they should occur. This will enable us to reach measured decisions on the appropriate management of each individual exposure.

This risk management guide gathers together contributions from experts in the management of different areas of risk. Their insights aim to help us all achieve a better understanding of our own risk profile and so manage it more effectively.

I am sure that you will find the guide to be a valuable working document.

ever feel like staying in bed?

Businesses and the directors who run them face a multitude of risks, says Stephen Womack, writer with the Financial Mail on Sunday. But identifying and managing risk is easier than you might think

We live in an uncertain world. In the past 12 months alone, one of the largest cities in the USA was devastated overnight by the power of nature; in London, terrorist attacks paralysed the city, shutting businesses and taking precious life; and, much of southern England was blanketed in a cloud of black smoke after the Buncefield oil storage terminal went up in flames.

Businesses, meanwhile, have seen their corporate identities stolen from Companies House, while individual employees have had their personal details taken from corporate records. Even the government has been caught out; it emerged last December that it had paid millions of pounds in fraudulent claims for Child Tax Credits, made possible because its own payroll data had been compromised and civil servants' National Insurance numbers were used to make bogus claims.

And, despite any politician's protests to the contrary, the mass of business legislation and red tape seems to be endlessly expanding. The dangers of falling victim to some obscure piece of environmental,

EXECUTIVE SUMMARY

- ☐ businesses operate in a world full of risk and uncertainty. These risks are constantly evolving and changing
- ☐ identifying and managing risk is still poorly understood as a business tool
- ☐ risk is an integral and necessary part of any good business
- ☐ companies that practice good risk management are more likely to survive and thrive

employment or competition legislation are rising. If your staff don't sue you, then your suppliers or customers might.

Directors sit at the centre of this maelstrom. Everyone has mornings when they'd rather stay in bed than face all the hazards the world can throw at them. But tucking your head under the covers is hardly a practical business strategy. You might be lucky in keeping your fingers crossed and hoping for the best. But those businesses that not only survive but also thrive do so because they understand risk.

Risk is actually a healthy part of business. Launching a new product, moving into a new market or making an acquisition can help a company grow. But it's important to recognise that each venture brings with it new risks that, if not handled properly, can also tip a business towards disaster.

The trick is to find cost-effective ways of reducing the likelihood of something going wrong or, in the event that it does, its impact on your business. Put another way, you need to manage the risks.

categorising risk

Risk is a little word that encompasses a multitude of dangers. And it means different things to different businesses, since a multinational can obviously absorb far more pain than an owner-managed company with a turnover of £2m. But the processes and techniques for assessing, reducing, eliminating or accepting risk are common to both.

Managing risk means thinking about it in a logical and structured way. Indeed, many of the companies that go under each year would have survived if they had faced up to risk properly.

Risk to a business can come from within, for example, through the actions of employees, the decisions of management, or the choice of its cash flow and accounting policies. There are also external threats – risks posed by factors beyond the control of the company or its directors.

Risk can be categorised under the following four headings: financial, strategic, operational and hazard. The table opposite sets out these risks in more detail.

TYPICAL DRIVERS OF BUSINESS RISK

	internal factors	external factors
financial risks	liquidity & cashflow	interest rates foreign exchange credit
strategic risks	research & development m&a integration	intellectual capital competition customer changes industry changes customer demand
operational risks	accounting controls IT systems recruitment supply chain	regulations culture board composition
hazard risks	employees properties public access products & services	contracts natural events suppliers environment

Source: The Risk Management Standard – IRM, Alarm & AIRMIC

Some risks have traditionally been given more attention than others. The danger of a factory burning down, for example, is a clear threat to the future of any business. Directors will have considered insurance, invested in alarms and sprinkler systems and had to comply with a raft of health and safety legislation.

Yet more subtle issues, such as overly generous credit terms for customers, lax internal accounting controls or a slight change in the market, may contain the seeds of a company's downfall. Many more businesses fail because of cash flow problems or bad debts than because their factory burns down. Both these risks can, and should, be managed.

the Risk Management Standard

Threats to a company are evolving all the time. Legislation changes, employees win new rights and new products and technology bring fresh challenges.

This means that directors have a duty to constantly monitor the risks they are running. Good corporate governance is no longer a luxury but a necessity, the lack of which could cause shareholders to take action.

The Risk Management Standard provides an overview of how to manage your business with risk in mind and sets out a list of duties for directors. It is published by the three risk management trade organisations: the Institute of Risk Management, Alarm and AIRMIC.

The Standard states that a board of directors should:

☐ know about the most significant risks facing the organisation

☐ know the possible effects on shareholder value of deviations to expected performance ranges

☐ ensure appropriate levels of awareness throughout the organisation

☐ know how the organisation will manage a crisis

☐ publish a clear risk management policy covering risk management philosophy and the responsibilities of senior management for perceived new risks or failures of existing control measures

But risk control is not solely about appeasing the shareholders and ticking boxes on a form. Effective control of risks can deliver tangible bottom line benefits. Reducing the number of workplace accidents or industrial illnesses, for example, should lead to a happier, healthier and more productive workforce, as well as lowering employers' liability insurance costs. (See the case study in chapter 4 for an excellent example of this.)

demystifying risk management

We manage risk every day, even if we don't consciously think about it. You lock your car – having first removed the SatNav system – look both ways before crossing the road, then de-activate the burglar alarm as you open up the office. Three separate examples of risk control before your first coffee of the morning.

A trite example, maybe, but nonetheless a useful illustration of how good we are at managing risks when the benefits of doing so are obvious. Most of us, though, could be even more risk-conscious. And most directors could implement risk management in their business in a way that makes the company stronger and their own personal position more secure.

Effective risk management requires you to understand your business intimately and to ask:

☐   how do different operations and processes interact?

☐   what if key facilities and people were not available?

☐   when would we be unable to operate?

☐   what if the unlikely and the unexpected actually happened?

According to the Risk Management Standard, the objective of risk management is: "To add maximum sustainable value to all the activities of the organisation. It marshals the understanding of the potential upside and downside of all those factors which can affect the organisation. It increases the probability of success, and reduces both the probability of failure and the uncertainty of achieving the organisation's overall objectives."

In short, risk management is good management. The following chapters in this guide will explain how to identify the threats and risks facing your business and how to plan to eliminate, reduce or transfer these risks.

new thinking for old problems

Thinking about old problems in a new way can help highlight the risks to your business, says Tim Kemp, deputy chief executive at HSBC Insurance Brokers

Directors are all aware in broad terms that their business faces risks and that something should be done to protect it from the consequences if these risks become a reality. However, the methodology of tackling risks and their management is not always obvious. Put another way, many of us know the 'what' of risk management but not the 'how'.

Some businesses are too small to justify a dedicated risk manager, leaving the task of managing risk to a senior member of the management team. Working out a practical approach to identifying risks and assessing them is not an easy task.

beyond the scope of a crystal ball

EXECUTIVE SUMMARY

- ☐ it's not always clear what your risks are and how to assess them
- ☐ using professional specialists can give you a new perspective
- ☐ identify those risks you can afford to live with, and the ones that could destroy the business
- ☐ try to eliminate or transfer those risks identified as 'fatal'

It is a misconception that most risks are predictable. Certainly some risks can be, but events can occur that are beyond the predictability of even risk management professionals. The 9/11 terrorist attacks in the USA are just one example.

We are now more aware of the risks posed by terrorism in general, but it is difficult to be specific about when and where these risks may occur, what their nature may be and the probable financial and commercial impact. As chapter 11 of the guide discusses, we all need to use our imaginations a little more.

Even the fallout from more predictable risks can also be hard to forecast. An example of this is the aftermath of the explosion at the Buncefield oil storage facility in Hertfordshire, in December, 2005. This particular incident highlights the need for effective business continuity planning that factors in not only those risks faced by your business, but also those of your neighbours that could affect you.

Internet clothing retailer ASOS was forced to suspend its shares after its only warehouse – located 700 metres from the oil facility – and its contents worth approximately £5m, were badly damaged. Later, the retailer stated that any lost profit and damage to assets would be covered by its insurance programme, and that it should still meet its full year profit forecast. This outcome illustrates the benefits of effective risk management practices and adequate insurance.

Major brands such as Dixons, Marks & Spencer and McDonalds were also affected as their factories close to the site in Hemel Hempstead were damaged.

The accident also resulted in the disruption to the supply of aviation fuel to London Heathrow Airport, which caused some airlines to pick up their passengers at Heathrow before flying to London Stansted Airport to refuel for transcontinental flights. See chapter 10 for more about planning to keep your business going in the face of such disruptions.

systematic and objective

A good starting point for any business looking to assess its risks is to break them down into different categories. As the table in chapter 1 shows (see page 11), they can be split into financial, operational, strategic and hazard risks.

If you lack the time or expertise in house to undertake this task, or are too close to your own business to see clearly the risks faced, many insurance brokers will provide risk management advice as part of their services in organising your insurance programme. Some of the larger practices, such as HSBC Insurance Brokers, have dedicated risk management professionals who will undertake this task either on a stand alone basis or as part of a wider package of services. Such experts can undertake a systematic mapping exercise of the risks your company faces, and provide advice about how to manage each individual risk.

risk aversion is relative

Once the risks are identified, each risk and its implications need to be properly understood and assessed.

When doing this, the business must take the strength of its balance sheet into account along with its own appetite for risk. Some businesses, and indeed some directors, are more risk averse than others.

Some risks can be managed and mitigated easily by updating or changing company policies; others may be accepted as a potential cost of doing business.

One exercise that can help this process is to set a series of 'pain thresholds' for your business. Each business will have its own thresholds, depending on its structure and turnover.

The following example is based on a company with a turnover of £2m:

- level 1 loss – £0 to £15k
  No problem. Up to this figure, the company can pay for the loss with a minimal impact on its cash, borrowing capacity or profits

- level 2 loss – £15k to £50k
  This hurts. The firm will survive but would be weakened. There could be an impact on investment and borrowing

- level 3 loss – £50k to £150k
  Potentially terminal. A loss of this magnitude leaves the company very weak, vulnerable and unable to absorb any more pain. Recovery is in doubt. Directors may lose control of their destiny

- level 4 loss – £150k or above
  This could trigger instant collapse. The company ceases trading

Clearly, some of the risks faced by a business will be deemed unacceptable. In the example above, level 3 and level 4 losses would definitely be, but so would some level 2 risks, depending on how frequently they occurred. These are the kind of risks that should be transferred to the insurance market, using the services of an insurance broker.

When deciding on insurance it is important to look beyond price and to remember that not all insurers are the same. Some provide products that offer different cover than others and some have different areas of speciality. All insurers have individual levels of service including claims handling. Some insurers have greater financial security – deeper pockets – than others.

However not all risks can be insured, and insurance is only one part of a good risk management programme. Prevention is always better than having to rely on having the right solution in place should an event occur.

A broker can help a business to navigate through these important areas of consideration in conjunction with the insurance and risk management programme design. There is no one-size-fits-all approach as every business is different. If a business faces specialist risks beyond the scope of your insurance adviser, he or she can bring in experts to assist in calculating the risks faced. For example, the assistance of auditors or forensic accountants may be required when assessing some financial risks, while marketing or brand experts may be helpful in assessing some aspects of business risk.

smart thinking is essential

With the increasing variety of risks posed by modern society, often a new way of looking at risk is required to ensure you have covered all your bases.

The potential for flu pandemics arising from avian flu is a prime example of the evolving world of risk. While the risks to poultry farmers are obvious, food manufacturers and retailers may also face very real risks to their supply chains.

Beyond the food sector, the risks may be less obvious. Yet many of the UK's largest organisations are planning for the eventuality of up to 25 per cent of their workforce becoming ill and incapacitated overnight. How would your business cope when faced with such circumstances? Threats such as avian flu and the Buncefield oil fire are clear reminders for businesses to have an up-to-date and adequate risk management and insurance programme that can give them maximum protection.

up close and personal

> Directors are paid to take tough decisions and also to bear the ultimate responsibility for their company. For the unwary, negligent or plain unlucky, carrying the can may mean a spell in prison, warns Stephen Womack

Directors are finding themselves in the firing line. Shareholders, employees, contractors and the authorities are increasingly keen to hold directors personally responsible for how they run a business.

This increase in risk is partly due to the creep of regulation. The more rules there are, the greater the chance you might break one of them. The increase is also due to better awareness and flows of information. Internet search engines, for example, can bring an entire library of employment law into the home of every disgruntled employee.

In some respects, the risks of being fined, disqualified or even imprisoned are simply part of the job. The responsibilities of being a director are what justify the high rewards. So, how can directors best manage these risks to ensure they enjoy their rewards in peace?

EXECUTIVE SUMMARY

- ☐ directors are often the target of litigation or enforcement action
- ☐ the number of regulations that may trip you up are increasing
- ☐ monitor legal developments and keep good records of the reasons for your decisions
- ☐ do not overlook the very real 'human' costs of being a director

there's good news and bad news

First the good – the law does not demand the impossible and the courts recognise the possibility that a director may make a genuine error or have been given poor advice. As the IoD's own *Director's Handbook* says: "Although the rules and regulations for directors have become more complex and onerous …there is no expectation of perfection or infallibility – all that the law requires is for the director to act honestly and competently."

Now for the bad. Too often problems arise because directors are confused about their role and duties. You need to be clear, both about your general position in law and about the specific role in a given business.

The latter will be determined by both the memorandum and articles of association, and by the wording of your service contract with a company, where such a written contract exists.

Do not discount the company's memorandum. A director could be sued by shareholders and held personally liable if he or she takes the business into areas that are not specified within the memorandum.

Common areas of confusion include:

☐ a conflict of interest – a director's duty is ultimately to the company and its shareholders, rather than to employees or to themselves. Directors must not favour majority shareholders over minority shareholders

☐ owner-managed companies – even where a director owns the majority or all of the shares in a company, duties to others, such as creditors, may override their personal interest

☐ delegation – if a director delegates a duty to another employee, the director remains liable for that duty

statutory duties

There are certain statutory obligations that bind all directors. Legislation in all these areas should be regularly monitored. While bigger companies may delegate the monitoring to a company secretariat or legal department, most directors in SMEs may have little choice but to keep watch themselves.

There is only space in this guide to give a taster, but the most important statutory duties include:

CUTTING THROUGH THE RED TAPE

Directors should find life a little less complicated thanks to the new Company Law Reform Act.

The Act removes the requirement for annual general meetings and company secretaries for private companies. It will allow companies to be formed online and will permit boards to meet by 'email'.

The government claims the measure will save business £250m a year in compliance costs.

The Act also restates, perhaps with more clarity than ever before, a director's duties. These include:

- a duty to promote the success of the company
- a duty to exercise independent judgement
- a duty to exercise reasonable care, skill and diligence
- a duty not to accept benefits from third parties

At the time of going to press, parliament was still debating this legislation, so there could be minor changes before it becomes law.

- **company law**

  The Companies Acts of 1985 and 1989 codify a director's legal duties in how a company is run and the individual's role and obligations. They outline some 250 offences; these split into administrative issues (filing annual accounts, company returns, etc.) and restrictions and expectations on the way directors should behave, for example, disclosing interests in shares, contracts and transactions. The Department for Trade & Industry publishes a series of Company Law Factsheets. Follow the web link www.dti.gov.uk/cld for more information. Some of the duties outlined in these acts are being replaced by the new Company Law Reform Act (see box above)

- **health and safety**

  The impact of legislation in this area will vary from business sector to business sector. But even the smallest company must by law follow at least ten procedures. Powers are wide ranging; no-one need be injured for a prosecution to take place and just the threat of a hazard is enough. Check for new measures at hse.gov.uk at least once a month. Chapter 4 discusses health and safety issues in more detail

- ☐ **environmental legislation**
  Government is keener than ever to be seen to be reducing business's impact on the environment. And this means extra legal duties for directors (see chapter 9)

- ☐ **competition law**
  This is a relatively new addition to the list of perils that can see a director imprisoned. Since 2003 directors can be deemed personally liable for some breeches of EU and UK competition law, with a maximum sentence of up to five years in prison

The courts can protect a director from legal action if they feel he or she has acted reasonably and with regard to all circumstances. A good example is where a director has taken advice from a professional such as an accountant or lawyer that later turns out to be incorrect.

THE HORROR OF COMPLACENCY

In September 2005, company director Paul White was sentenced to 12 months in prison after one of his employees died in a workplace accident.

White ran MW White, a paper recycling firm based in Ketteringham, Norwich. Employee Kevin Arnup was killed three days before Christmas in 2003.

The dry language of the HSE's report masks the true horror of Kevin Arnup's death. "Mr Arnup climbed into a paper-shredding machine to clear blockages when the machine started, fatally injuring him. The machine contained a series of hammers projecting 15cm from a shaft, which revolved at high speed."

There was no way to isolate the machine from the electricity supply to prevent it starting, and no safe system to clear blockages.

White pleaded guilty to manslaughter and health and safety charges. The company had to pay a £30,000 fine, and costs of £55,000 were split between White and the business.

Why highlight this case? Not only was the accident 'entirely foreseeable' and 'totally preventable', according to the HSE, but it was compounded by complacency; having called in a health and safety consultant to advise on best practice, White chose to not to follow that advice. Instead, he carried on the business in what the HSE described as 'a complacent manner'.

The message here: once any risk has been identified, directors fail to act on it at their – and their employees' – peril.

The lesson here? Try to pick good advisers obviously but, above all, keep records of their advice, and full minutes of every meeting and board decision.

you're not alone

Directors, of course, can make some safeguards against the costs and distress of stumbling in one of their duties. The Companies (Audit, Investigations and Community Enterprise) Act 2004 changed the rules on how companies can help directors defend themselves.

From April 2005 it relaxed many prohibitions on companies indemnifying directors against liability and has allowed companies to pay defence costs as they are incurred, regardless of the outcome of the case.

The other option is to buy commercial directors' and officers' insurance. Such D&O cover is designed to pay towards defending directors from actions against them.

Each policy is different and your broker can help tailor the right package for you.

Both the board collectively and directors thinking of their own position should make time to read the details of any proposed insurance carefully. Check who is covered, for what roles and duties, whether joint venture projects are included, how long cover extends after a director has resigned and how quickly it comes into force where the business makes an acquisition.

Insurance is usually a wise option – indeed, best practice on corporate governance recommends it – but it is not a panacea.

risks to you and your lifestyle

There is another type of risk that is all too easily overlooked. Directors are human beings too, with all the usual physical frailties and emotional needs. Only you can look after these needs by:

- making time for regular health checks
- getting away from the desk. In this era of mobile phones, laptops and

BlackBerries, work has a habit of finding you wherever you are

- [ ] being aware of the dangers of stress. Studies by the International Stress Management Association have found that directors and owner-managers are some of the most stressed in the workplace. Chapter 4 has more information on combating stress

- [ ] not leaving yourself isolated. Management can be lonely, especially in smaller operations. Some may dismiss organisations such as Rotary or Chambers of Commerce as old-fashioned, but getting involved can give you a valuable support network

Finally, consider your family. One study earlier this year found one-third of senior managers would cancel a family holiday if they felt it would help clinch an important contract. More than half were prepared to forgo a wedding anniversary dinner for the same reason. There are no hard and fast rules in this area but, speaking bluntly, if you find you are always putting work ahead of family maybe you should ask yourself if you're in the right job?

are you taking risks with your staff?

Looking after your workforce in the right way is key to reducing the human risks of being in business, says Nic Paton, journalist specialising in workplace issues and news editor at Occupational Health magazine

Employees today have more workplace rights than ever before. They may be your greatest asset but, arguably, they are also your greatest liability.

The workplace is now covered by various laws banning all discrimination on the grounds of religion or sexual orientation. These complement long-standing anti-discrimination laws on race and gender.

Working parents or those caring for relatives have won new rights to extra maternity and paternity leave and flexible working. The European Working Time Directive has limited the working week to 48 hours in all but a very few professions.

EXECUTIVE SUMMARY

- [ ] workers have more rights – and are more willing to exert them
- [ ] risk management strategies need to reflect the changing nature of workplace 'injuries'
- [ ] absence costs employers more than £12bn a year
- [ ] investing in rehabilitation and retraining for employees can more than pay for itself

In October 2006, laws will come into force that will ban age discrimination in the workplace. Many employment lawyers have predicted that these will in time fundamentally change how workplaces operate, as well as how people are recruited and managed, and how and when they retire.

These are all risks that need to be addressed by directors (see also chapter 7). But when it comes to employee risk management, perhaps the biggest day-to-day

INDUSTRIAL ILLNESS AND ABSENCE TRENDS

According to the Health and Safety Executive:

- two million people suffered from work-related ill health in 2004/05 – 200,000 fewer than in 2001/02
- fatal injuries fell by seven per cent, or 220 deaths in 2004/05, compared with 236 the previous year
- reported major injuries to employees (mostly slips and trips) were down 2.2 per cent to 30,213
- stress and musculoskeletal disorders account for around two-thirds of all occupational ill health
- one in five workers finds their work very or extremely stressful
- each case of stress-related workplace ill-health results in an average of 28 days lost employment

According to the CBI:

- workplace absence cost UK plc £12.2bn in 2004 – up from £11.6bn
- the direct cost of absence (paying salaries, arranging cover and lost productivity) was £495 per employee

challenge faced by many small and medium-sized businesses is that of absence through illness or injury.

absence costs hurt business

In hard statistical terms, industrial illness and absence trends are improving (see box above). This is partly because companies are getting better at managing the health and safety of their workers, motivated by the ever-more stringent regulatory regime. It is also because fewer workers are being employed in more dangerous industries.

Nonetheless, when you look at the cost of work-related absence and illness, it is clear that this is an area that no employer – small or large – can afford to ignore.

The Confederation of British Industry (CBI) and health insurer AXA publish one of the best-respected surveys in this area annually. It suggests the total cost to the economy of workplace absence was £12.2bn in 2004, and the figure is rising.

MANAGING DOWN ACCIDENTS

Copper tubing manufacturer Yorkshire Copper Tube has cut its employers' liability insurance premium by £500,000 and seen a 30 per cent reduction in days lost since it implemented a new health and safety programme in 2003.

The review was prompted by a rise in insurance costs after the business changed ownership.

"In the past 12 months the number of accidents has fallen from 22 to 12, and, unlike in 2004 when we had two big incidents, all of them have been fairly minor," says Paul Smith, the company's plant manager.

This reduction has been achieved through a number of measures, including:

☐ consultation with staff on risks and possible solutions

☐ 'toolbox talks' to encourage workers to report hazards

☐ a new inspection and maintenance regime and a new dedicated cleaning team for communal areas and gangways

Every accident is reviewed and, if needed, an inquiry held. This year the company plans to introduce weekly meetings with team leaders to discuss any issues.

If someone is injured, there is access to an occupational health nurse during the day and a doctor every fortnight. There are first aiders on each shift and the security team are all trained in first aid.

"It is worth talking to other organisations that have started the process – we went through the HSE website," says Smith.

"We have had to spend money, but this has often been on things we would have had to invest in anyway, such as improving the floor. It is not just the fact that people are not absent, you also get a payback in improved morale," he adds.

The CBI stresses that taking action and being proactive can make a significant difference. Where senior managers (as opposed to line managers only) are actively involved absence rates can improve dramatically.

Monitoring absence is essential, it says. This means logging the causes and investigating why people are taking time off. It is also important to recognise that good health and safety and absence management need not cost the earth.

While bigger companies will normally be able to draw on the expertise of a human resources or occupational health department, for smaller companies it may be more appropriate and cost effective simply to ensure that someone at board level takes responsibility for managing employment, health and welfare issues.

The best model is likely to be a few well-communicated, formal policies, for instance, on recruitment, discrimination, calling in sick and return to work, backed by a culture of ongoing, informal, constructive communication.

Among some of the better resources available, the Association of Insurance and Risk Managers (AIRMIC) and the CBI last year published two booklets on rehabilitating workers as part of an ongoing campaign to encourage businesses to take a more active role in helping sick or injured staff back to work.

The Chartered Institute of Personnel and Development publishes regular guidance on managing absence. The manufacturers' body EEF, too, has been active in pulling together a range of online tools and guides.

industrial diseases are changing

Knowing how to respond to, say, a chemical spill is relatively easy, compared with conditions such as stress, repetitive strain injury (RSI), and musculo-skeletal disorders (MSD) such as back pain.

Stress is not even a medical condition (although depression and anxiety, which will often be stress-related, can be). Similarly RSI, which is often bandied around workplaces, is a catch-all term for a range of disorders.

Stress also affects people in different ways – a situation or environment that one person finds stressful can be hugely stimulating and motivational to another. There may be factors in the worker's home life that need to be taken into account, too.

Staff questionnaires – where responses are anonymous – can be a good starting point for identifying any stress 'hotspots'. Examining departmental absence and staff turnover records for any stress, MSD or general absence trends can also prove helpful.

Once someone is off sick it is important to maintain communication, despite this being something many managers feel nervous about for fear of being thought of as intrusive or harassing a worker.

The EEF estimates that one million people go off sick every day. After six months 3,000 of them are still off, and 80 per cent of those will not come back to work for the next five years. It is worth looking at whether you can modify your workplace so that even if someone is not 100 per cent fit they can still come back and be involved, perhaps in a different role or part-time at first.

combating stress at work

Earlier this year the Health and Safety Executive launched The Better Business campaign, targeting SMEs and encouraging them to take health and safety and staff wellbeing more seriously.

Tackling stress effectively is often as much about changing cultures and attitudes as it is about amending processes and rules. In 2004, the HSE developed a series of management standards for tackling stress to help employers identify the primary sources of stress within their organisation. It categorises these 'stressors' into six key areas:

- ☐ demands (workload, work patterns, work environment)
- ☐ how much control and say someone has over their work
- ☐ the amount of support they get
- ☐ their relationships at work
- ☐ their role
- ☐ how change is managed within the business

The idea is that you measure how your organisation is doing against the standards and then follow the advice on what strategies to take.

It can take as long as 18 months or more for the benefits from any stress reduction programme to filter through. Companies should be prepared to take lots of small steps to achieve change rather than trying to implement an ambitious programme in one fell swoop, suggests the HSE.

Being able to show you are actively following or implementing the HSE stress management standards should also help when it comes to defending any claim in a tribunal or court of law.

keeping the cash flowing

Cash keeps the business heart pumping, but if there's a blockage the company can die. Chris Wheal, business and insurance journalist, suggests a healthy regime to reduce the risk of financial heart attacks

Bad debt does not discriminate; it can infect the biggest companies as well as the smallest. Remember when you ate crisps made by Golden Wonder and you bought furniture in Allders? These, and other recent high-profile collapses by household-name companies, have rammed home the message that having blue-chip customers no longer guarantees a rosy future.

A long-term contract tying a supplier to a major name used to be seen by many as a financial security blanket. Nowadays, it is regarded as potentially suffocating. If you've sacrificed other customers to fulfil the demands of your biggest buyer, will you survive if that giant is slain?

EXECUTIVE SUMMARY

- ☐ monitor and review your own credit control and invoicing procedures
- ☐ consider tailoring credit terms for each individual customer
- ☐ credit insurance and factoring can help to keep the money moving
- ☐ be aware of costs that can escalate suddenly and make a plan to manage these risks

no guarantees

The reality of running a modern business is that there are no financial guarantees. Every sale, every customer and every supplier comes with some risks. The best-run companies identify those risks, reduce them where possible and plan ways of coping when a risk turns into a reality.

securing prompt payment

Perhaps the first financial risk to examine is the last one in the chain – getting paid on time. More businesses go under because of late payment than because of non-payment. Their cash simply runs out while they wait for their buyer to put that infamous cheque in the post.

Good credit management systems and practices are essential – and the Institute of Credit Management claims that companies with good credit management practices have better management across the board.

Good credit management starts with assessing potential new customers before agreeing a sale and then re-assessing them – even the blue-chip firms – at least twice a year. Any changes in demand or payment times need a full explanation.

Best practice is to give each customer their own credit terms – not necessarily 30 days across the board – and make those terms clear in writing, with any changes also communicated explicitly.

This should be done before agreeing any sale, not afterwards, and based on proper credit checking, using commercial agencies, trade association information and your own business grapevine.

Invoices need to be sent on time, in the format acceptable to the client, including any relevant purchase order numbers, and they should be addressed to the right person (not necessarily the individual who placed the order). If you do not get these basics right, a customer has lots of excuses to delay payment.

credit as a business tool

All sorts of actions can affect the length of credit period that you will agree to for each individual client or for each individual sale. Late payment by a client may result in you cutting that customer's credit period, for example.

Research from the Credit Management Research Centre (CMRC) at Leeds University found companies also extended credit periods to attract new customers, to cope with changes in a customer's risk profile, to gain exports and even to shift slow-moving products.

There is a trend for major companies to demand longer credit periods from their suppliers. Retail groups Tesco and Halfords have hit the headlines for their new payment policies, for example.

The Better Payments Practice Group is opposed to companies forcing longer periods on their suppliers. It recommends that the decision to extend credit terms should be agreed at face-to-face meetings and always be based on improved risk. It also advises companies to plan ahead by researching the other party, setting objectives and identifying possible concessions to help negotiate less intimidating changes.

Always, always negotiate. Don't just accept it, especially if you cannot afford the cost of the borrowing you need to fund the extended credit period.

insurance solutions

Even with the best system, some clients may still go under owing you money. Your business may be spread widely enough to afford the loss of one customer but many companies will need every penny. A solution here could be credit insurance – and now is a good time to buy because many more insurers are offering this type of cover, so prices are keen.

An additional advantage of buying credit insurance is the access to risk and credit-rating information on your customers that the insurer will provide for you. They have mountains of information to help them price the risks and this could help you decide who to trade with and on what terms, especially when looking for new customers or export markets.

Evidence suggests having creditor insurance improves companies' credit management internally. More than three-quarters of companies reported to the CMRC that using credit insurance had influenced the terms they offered.

If this all sounds like a lot of hassle diverting you from your core business skills, or you realise you must offer credit periods but actually need the cash earlier, there are outsourcing and financing options available. These can either run your invoicing and credit control for you or lend you the money against your invoices (see box on page 35 on invoice discounting and factoring).

CONTROLLING THE RISKS OF GROWTH

Birmingham-based plastic carrier-bag maker Euro Packaging has used credit insurance since 1986. At first the company's bank insisted it get cover to guarantee its overdraft. But in the past four years Afzal Majid, joint managing director, says his business has benefited from the proactive approach of his insurance broker.

Early information on changes in credit risk and fast decisions on potential new customers, based on extensive local knowledge in far-flung foreign parts, has enabled Euro Packaging to become an international giant.

The company, which has factories as far apart as China and Malaysia, has seen its turnover grow from under $1m in 1986 to $400m today. It now sells bags to retailers in Russia, eastern Europe, France, Australia, New Zealand and the US – from Carrefour to Walmart.

"If they say a credit risk is not acceptable then we don't trade. But because they have the local knowledge we can make a decision quickly," says Mr Majid.

And because HSBC Insurance Brokers' local contacts are constantly letting the company know about improvements in credit risks, as well as worsening risks, Euro Packaging has been able to take advantage of opportunities early. "Sometimes we take a different profile on a risk but when we get cover we have been able to trade more robustly," he says.

external price shocks

Not all the risks are at the point of sale. A sudden rise in any of your raw material charges, energy costs or other input prices can also cause shockwaves, especially if passing on those costs to your customers is not possible because of contractual obligations or market pressure.

One big hitter in terms of whacking input costs in recent years has been energy charges. Wars, fires, and farmers and lorry drivers blockading refineries have all played their part in causing panic buying at the petrol pumps. Meanwhile wobbles in the gas supply last winter saw some big industrial users having the tap turned off.

The biggest energy users have full-time staff to manage their supply costs, hedging prices and negotiating tailored contracts. But energy suppliers will offer fixed price contracts to smaller users too.

Planning is the key here, especially for small to medium-sized companies that lack the buying clout to negotiate with suppliers when prices start to rise, according

FACTORING AND INVOICE DISCOUNTING

Both services normally provide finance against invoices you have sent but not yet been paid for. Factoring gives the extra benefit of running your full sales ledger and collections service for you, chasing up invoices and collecting outstanding debts.

Under an invoice discounting service, by contrast, you continue to administer the sales ledger and the service is usually undisclosed to customers. Invoice discounters will typically fund about 80 per cent of your invoice value immediately, profiting by taking the full price later and running the risk of defaults.

There are two types of factoring – recourse and non-recourse factoring. Recourse factoring excludes bad debt protection. The risk remains with you and if the customer fails to pay, the factor will look to you to repay the amount financed against that debt.

If bad debt protection is included, the service is called non-recourse factoring. This means that if a credit-approved customer fails to pay an undisputed debt, the factor will credit you with the amount of the debt.

to the Institute of Purchasing and Supply. That means monitoring price predictions and getting orders in early that will match your needs. But it also means making sure that you can benefit from any price reductions that might feed through later – remember prices can come down as well as go up. And with sudden price rises often indicating a risk that supply may actually be cut off completely, the best planning will involve ensuring the security of supply and not just the price.

It is better to be secure and allow for that in your selling price, informing your customer and winning the business on the basis of your reliability, than to appear the cheapest and be first to go to the wall when the chips are down.

Ignoring the financial risks can be hugely costly, but a bit of planning, a little foresight and some extra effort put in to the unglamorous, sometimes tediously administrative side of your business can make all the difference between success and failure.

minimising M&A risks

> The right advice and specialist forms of cover can take some of the risk out of a sale or acquisition, says Alena Watchorn, head of corporate finance insurance services at HSBC Insurance Brokers

The sale or purchase of a company carries the greatest opportunities in business, but also some of the greatest risks. For smaller companies, in particular, the wrong acquisition can kill the business. The right deal, though, is a springboard to greater heights.

Any merger or acquisition will carry strategic risks. Is this the correct market to be entering or exiting? Is the price of the deal right? Will there be a cultural fit? The table on page 11 in chapter 1 rightly lists M&A risks as one category to put on your checklist.

What can be overlooked, though, are the personal exposures that directors may be required to assume in any deal. These can come both in the role of a board member, but also where the director is a significant shareholder in the business.

EXECUTIVE SUMMARY

- directors can be held personally liable for problems that emerge from the woodwork after a business is sold
- buyers also need protection, not least if the sellers don't have deep pockets
- transactional risks can be reduced by using a range of specialist insurance covers
- be wary of buying a series of past liabilities along with the ongoing business

the role of warranties

Buyers will conduct thorough due diligence based on the information provided to them through the sellers' disclosure. But a residual risk remains that something will emerge that nobody knew about that reduces the value of the business. As a result, buyers often require personal warranties from the shareholders and/or the directors of the selling company to ensure that all relevant information has been revealed through disclosure documents related to the sale. Typically, the terms of any such warranties – effectively promises – are negotiated by the lawyers representing both the buyers and sellers, and form part of the allocation of risk between the parties.

insurance solutions

Protecting warranties should form an integral part of the risk management of any transaction. Insurance can be arranged to cover these warranties and is designed to provide protection for either seller or buyer from unknown and undisclosed losses that could impact after the sale.

Typically, the warranties required by a buyer would cover share ownership, litigation, accounts, and IT – in short, anything that could affect the value of the business they are buying. These warranties give the buyer the right to sue shareholders of the selling business should a nasty surprise emerge in the future.

Insurance bought by the sellers of a business protects them from claims made by the buyer under the warranty, and the costs of defending an alleged breach of warranty. This is provided the claim is as a result of innocent, rather than deliberate, non-disclosure on the part of the seller.

Insurance brokers can arrange the purchase of warranty insurance for either buyers or sellers to protect them if the warranty is called upon. They can also provide advice on the structure of such insurance and its pricing, place the request for cover in the market and finally coordinate and oversee the purchasing of cover.

Warranty insurance can also provide additional comfort to buyers. This particularly applies in cases where the selling shareholders: are overseas; are financially insecure; or have capped their exposures to a low level.

Buyers will also look for insurance where the majority shareholder in the selling company is an institutional investor, who would typically not provide warranties.

While the minority shareholders – typically, management shareholders – will probably provide personal warranties, these would be capped to the level of their shareholding, and the buyer may wish to purchase top-up warranty insurance to protect their exposure to the rest of their acquisition.

HIDDEN RISKS

Pollution and contaminated land liability is an increasing risk in mergers and acquisitions, particularly where the seller has operated industrial or manufacturing activities in the past.

This is mainly due to tightening environmental regulation and the strict enforcement of historical pollution clean-up responsibilities.

In the UK, for example, the Environmental Protection Act 1990 puts an obligation on local authorities to seek out and remediate land affected by pollution. Where there are pollution problems, they would normally pursue the original polluter, eg. a landfill operator or a foundry owner. Where the original polluter cannot be found or has gone out of business, the liability may pass to the current landowner.

It is also common for such liabilities to be negotiated and transferred contractually to other companies or individuals via warranties and indemnities given during corporate transactions involving the affected land.

Brokers can assist both sellers and buyers with assessing the likelihood of such risks, the need for due diligence and advising as to where liability lies. Specialist environmental impairment liability insurance can be purchased to protect against pollution and contaminated land liability.

protection in the City

Personal warranties from directors are also often required for an investment or subscription agreement. This is particularly pertinent to cases where a business is receiving a significant cash injection – for example, from venture capitalists – or is selling a minority shareholding to an investment house or venture capital firm.

Initial public offerings (IPOs) on the stock market can also create a need for insurance cover. Directors assume personal liability for the accuracy of the information provided in IPO documents, such as prospectuses, and can arrange for specialised prospectus liability insurance that will ring fence their liability for that document.

Investment banks, sponsors, or issue underwriters involved in selling shares in an IPO may seek warranties in the event that they get involved in a claim arising from a mis-statement or error in the prospectus.

The initial risk management involved in a merger or acquisition transaction is typically undertaken by investment houses, accountants or lawyers. Insurance brokers are also often involved early in the process in advising on the ability to structure insurance to assist a clean exit for shareholders, or to enhance the protection available for a potential bidder for the business.

WARRANTY INSURANCE LIMITS SELLERS' LIABILITIES

International engineering company Dickens was formed from a leveraged management buy-out from a publicly traded company in 2002. The buy-out was carried out by its management, senior employees and institutional investors.

The institutional shareholders were keen to realise their investment as Dickens had grown and they believed they could obtain a significant profit from selling their shares.

The directors were aware that the buyers would require access to detailed information about the company. They were also conscious that if such information did not fully and fairly reflect the position of the company, they may be expected to provide personal warranties.

The institutional shareholders had made it clear that they would not assume any liability for warranties relating to the business. As a result, the full burden lay with the directors.

To manage and mitigate the potential risks, and to attract potential buyers, the sellers and their advisers prepared an information memorandum, and conducted some due diligence. This included:

- [ ] financial due diligence conducted by their accountants

- [ ] assessing historical contamination from previous use that might have existed

- [ ] insurance due diligence of the company's existing insurance and risk management protection

Potential buyers were asked to submit their bids based on this preliminary information. The eventual buyers still insisted on personal warranties from the management shareholders to protect them from unknown, undisclosed risks, and an environmental indemnity to protect against the potential risk of a claim or regulatory clean-up requirement in relation to one site.

To manage this risk, the management shareholders not only provided extensive disclosure but also sought, through their lawyers, to negotiate limitations to such risks.

Ultimately, it was recognised that the management shareholders of the company would remain liable to the buyer for some risk, albeit capped at the value of their shareholding (20 per cent). They bought insurance protection in the form of warranty insurance for this exposure.

For example, if the sellers include institutional investors who are unwilling to provide warranties, the management shareholders/directors may choose to seek advice at an early stage over the insurance options available to protect their position and manage their risk.

Brokers can also conduct due diligence on the level of risk management in the target company generally, on the levels of other types of insurance cover already in place, and on the potential for future claims to emerge (see box on hidden risks, page 39). These facts help inform negotiations.

keeping on the right side of the law

Carrying out regular risk assessments can help a business avoid breaking the law, say Margaret Coltman and James Bagge, partners with law firm Norton Rose

The legal burden of being in business is fast-changing and ever-growing. The spectacular growth in the rules, laws, directives and regulations that apply to modern businesses has continued to increase. According to a recent survey carried out by MORI on behalf of International HR consultancy DDI, the worst thing about being a business leader in the UK is keeping pace with legislation.

Some of these changes relate to specific types of business, but many of them apply to all UK businesses. How can directors keep track of all these changes? How can they minimise the risk of not doing so? Many businesses are also affected by laws outside the UK through cross-border trade. Those that ignore local laws and practices do so at their peril.

EXECUTIVE SUMMARY

- [ ] the volume of business regulation is growing
- [ ] it is a duty of directors to keep up to date with the rules: ignorance is not a defence
- [ ] the cost and time involved in defending an action can be as damaging as a claim itself
- [ ] businesses need to assess the risks of litigation and develop written plans of how they should respond

where the red tape is growing

Laws govern all aspects of business. Employees have an increasing number of rights in relation to employment and pensions, as well as health and safety.

Environmental laws regulate not only the storage of products but how goods are manufactured and packaged, and how waste is dealt with. Data protection laws govern how information is stored and how it can be used.

new laws affecting the workplace

UK workplace discrimination laws have undergone significant change over recent years. Laws outlawing discrimination on the grounds of sexual orientation, religion or belief and disability will be joined on 1 October 2006 by new regulations that will ban age discrimination in employment and vocational training.

The new regulations will prohibit retirement ages below 65, except where objectively justified, and will remove the current upper age limit of 65 from unfair dismissal and redundancy rights. Employers will have to consider an employee's request to continue working beyond retirement. Businesses will need to put in place appropriate policies to deal with these changes and, if necessary, change their organisational structure to provide for them.

Employers will need to ensure they actively discourage age-related banter or any other behaviour by individual employees that could be seen as evidence of an ageist working culture. All contractual terms and conditions should be checked, and application and recruitment procedures audited, for compliance. As with other areas where discrimination in employment can occur, ongoing monitoring may be effective in order to defend any allegations of discrimination that are made.

New laws are also planned to improve the life of working parents. The Work and Families Bill, published in October 2005, is intended to extend rights to maternity leave and pay. Working mothers will be able to transfer part of the rights to fathers, and the current rights of parents with young children to request flexible working arrangements will be extended from April 2007 to those caring for sick or elderly relatives.

health and safety

The Health and Safety Executive (HSE) implements all health and safety legislation across the UK. Following a successful prosecution, the courts then decide on what penalties to impose. In response to failures to achieve targeted reductions in the incidence of fatal and major work-related injuries, the HSE has said it believes that the general level of fines does not properly reflect the seriousness of health and safety offences. Consequently, businesses can expect to see an increase in the maximum fines that can be imposed and, in serious cases, imprisonment of offenders.

The proposed Corporate Manslaughter Bill will create a new statutory offence addressing particularly serious safety management failures resulting in death. Pressure is strong for there to be some form of individual culpability attached to a new corporate offence.

packaging, waste and recycling

Much of UK environmental law is based on EU directives. Businesses need to be aware of likely changes so that they can allocate resources and, if necessary, modify processes to meet the new requirements.

For example, changes have been announced to the Producer Responsibility Obligations (Packaging Waste) Regulations 1997, which require producers to register their packaging, recover it and recycle it. Consultation took place during 2005 on options to increase the amount of packaging covered by the regulations, to include leased packaging, such as pallets and crates, as well as packaging handled by franchisors and their franchisees. Consultation also took place during the year on how to meet the higher recovery and recycling targets set by the EU Packaging and Packaging Waste Directive, for achievement by 2008.

ignorance is no defence

It is essential that companies keep track of their duties and obligations. There is no magic formula as to how to achieve this. It requires the allocation of time and resource.

The internet offers businesses valuable access to numerous websites with details of relevant law and regulation. Many bodies offer subscriptions to email alert services.

The DTI provides information about employment laws at www.dti.gov.uk/er/index.htm. The Disability Rights Commission website www.drc.org.uk is useful for laws relating to disability, and data protection requirements can be found on the Information Commissioner's website www.informationcommissioner.gov.uk.

Information sources on health and safety laws are discussed in chapter 4 and on environmental legislation in chapter 9.

Other ways of keeping abreast of changes and remaining in compliance are:

- ensuring that someone is made responsible for keeping up to date with changes and given the time to do the work required. Task them with training and ensuring management and employees are aware of new issues

- using the information provided by trade bodies. Organisations such as the Federation of Small Businesses, which lobbies government on behalf of small businesses, provides useful briefs on numerous legal issues that affect their members. Another comprehensive information resource is www.businesslink.gov.uk

- using professional advice, for example, from accountants, lawyers, insurance brokers and risk assessment consultants. It is their job to keep up to date with changes and they will often be able to point you in the right direction

risk of failing to comply

Litigation is on the increase and businesses are being subjected to a wide range of claims. For many businesses, reputation is arguably their greatest asset. Litigation can be highly damaging to a company's reputation. It is also expensive, a drain on management resources and can even bring a business down.

The Shell case is a high profile example of what can happen when things start to go wrong (see box on page 45).

minimising the risk of litigation

By carrying out regular risk assessments, a business can analyse the risks it faces from potential litigation or claims and can decide how to reduce the risk involved.

CAN YOU BE SURE OF SHELL?

In January 2004, the Royal Dutch/Shell group of companies announced that it was recategorising 3.9bn 'barrels of oil equivalent' of its proved hydrocarbon reserves (20 per cent of its then proved reserves). Shell's share price fell substantially; on the day of that first announcement alone its market capitalisation fell by some £2.9bn.

By mid-April, following further announcements, the total recategorisation stood at about 4.3bn 'barrels of oil equivalent'. The US Department of Justice, the Securities and Exchange Commission (SEC) and the Financial Services Authority (FSA) all commenced investigations.

Shell's chairman, finance director, and head of exploration and production operations resigned. Without admitting liability, Shell settled with the SEC for US$120m and with the FSA for £17m. It also agreed to commit a further US$5m to develop and implement a comprehensive internal compliance programme which has resulted in a fundamental reorganisation of the Shell group's corporate structure. The FSA's separate action into Shell's chairman, Sir Philip Watts, was dismissed.

However, Shell is still the subject of a substantial US class action alleging securities fraud.

A risk assessment will focus on risks specific to the business. A business that is dominant in its market will need to ensure that its trading practices do not amount to an abuse of its dominant position. A business that works for public or government authorities must ensure that its practices are not at risk of being seen as bribes.

When carrying out risk assessments:

☐ ensure that the hazards of the business are identified. Decide what you can reasonably do to avoid or reduce the risk. If you rely on contracts, review them to assess how robust they are

☐ decide what steps you need to take in response to the magnitude of the risk. Make sure your reporting lines are appropriate and that you have effective systems and controls in place

☐ draw up codes of conduct, so that your managers and employees understand what is required of them. Make it a condition of their employment that they abide by them

☐ train your staff in your methods and test your incident management systems. Managers, employees and agents need to understand what they are expected to do

☐ keep your risk assessment up to date. Review it regularly and check your internal policies and procedures to ensure that they take account of your findings

☐ obtain professional advice, so that you can be sure you have covered the ground thoroughly

By taking these steps you will be in a much better position to anticipate problems so that you can be pro-active if the worst happens.

coping in a crisis

No business is immune from a critical incident. It could be a legal claim, an industrial accident, an employee fraud or an investigation by a regulator. What a business can do, however, is to make sure that proper steps are in place to address a crisis when it occurs. Contingency plans should include:

☐ an internal decision-making matrix, identifying how a team is appointed to manage a crisis and allocating responsibility for dealing with it

☐ an internal and external communications plan, with contact details and clear procedures for communicating with staff, suppliers, customers and the press. The flow of information must be managed if the damage that could be caused by the crisis is to be contained

☐ an investigation plan, including procedures for identifying the issues, the further risks involved and the review of evidence

☐ a document management plan

If the worst happens, you will need to implement these plans. Among the actions they will require are to:

☐ notify your insurers. You may not be able to claim if you have prejudiced their position

☐ collect the facts whilst the incident is still fresh in people's minds, but do so in a systematic and controlled way and with professional legal help where appropriate (see panel on the next page)

WHAT IF? THE IMPORTANCE OF LEGAL PRIVILEGE

A company issues its results to the market. The announcement contains inaccuracies. The board tasks one of the directors with the job of finding out what went wrong. Together with the internal auditors he presents a written report to the board and the company issues a corrective announcement. The share price falls and the FSA tells the company it wants to investigate suspected market abuse. It requests copies of internal or external audit reports. As the report to the board was not prepared by a lawyer or in contemplation of litigation, it is not privileged and the company has no option but to hand it over.

- ☐ retain all documents and electronic data. Even accidental destruction can lead to adverse inferences

- ☐ take professional advice. Do not try to defend a claim on your own

- ☐ check that new documents that are created will not damage your case

Finally, keep on top of the claim and the issues. Ensure that you respond promptly to questions, particularly from regulators. In an ever-regulated environment, failure to do so can expose a business to unacceptable risk.

the fight against fraud

Fraud and dishonesty in the workplace cost business billions of pounds a year. Martin Schramm, head of commercial crime insurance at Zurich Global Corporate UK, outlines steps companies can take to stamp out this white-collar crime

Burglar alarms, security grills, razor wire and CCTV – these 21st century additions to the exteriors of factories, shops and offices show that businesses are all too aware of the threat that burglars and arsonists pose. But these measures are no longer enough to ensure complete protection.

EXECUTIVE SUMMARY

- ☐ fraud can threaten a company's liquidity

- ☐ insurance products cover the direct financial loss arising out of dishonest acts

- ☐ cases involving organised crime, 'sleepers' and 'cloning' are a new dimension to internal fraud

- ☐ with adequate controls in place the impact of fraud and dishonesty can be limited

Today's criminals are finding there are better ways to steal from a business than sneaking around in the middle of the night with a stocking over their head. Directors need to be alert to growing threats such as fraud and deception.

Often dismissed as victimless crimes, deception and fraud are anything but. It's not just companies that lose money: if they go out of business as a result, then employees may be out of a job. And customers can be left struggling if their suppliers are not able to deliver due to financial difficulties through fraud.

the rise of fraud

The incidence of internal fraud and dishonesty appears to be increasing but because businesses are often reluctant to report the crime, accurate figures are hard to determine. According to accountants RSM Robson Rhodes the total impact of economic crime in the UK is estimated to be £3.4bn annually. A survey conducted by consultants PWC in 2005 places dishonesty, deception and money laundering as the top three fraud threats as perceived by companies in Europe. However, although 54 per cent of the companies are subject to dishonest acts, only 22 per cent of company directors believe internal fraud to be the major threat to their business.

The uncomfortable truth is that the perpetrators are often trusted employees. Both PWC and consultants KPMG have found that the majority of 'inside jobs' are executed by middle management or subordinates. The experience of Zurich shows that small and remote subsidiaries are often the place where fraud is most likely to be committed.

financial consequences of fraud

Internal fraud and dishonesty is commonly insured. Cover will usually pay any direct financial losses. But additional costs incurred conducting fraud investigations and prosecutions, or contractual penalties and other consequential losses suffered by a company, may not be insurable.

Deception and financial misrepresentation are not in themselves insurable. But financial losses following the acceptance of forged documents, counterfeit money and securities is widely covered by the crime products of the major insurers. Most will pay out if an electronic funds transfer is triggered by hackers. However, proving that this has happened might be difficult.

Treasury, funds transfers and loans are areas where fraud has the highest potential impact on a company's cash position. Robust controls and the segregation of duties during reconciliation processes are therefore important methods to prevent the most obvious threat of internal fraud.

controls reduce the risks

Interestingly, the perceived risk of incurring losses through computer fraud appears to be higher than the actual number of losses reported. But this fact should not give cause for complacency. The following good practice measures are worth adopting:

- [ ] dual controls offer a good level of protection, especially with dealing, funds transfer and loans. The use of Electronic Funds Transfer (EFT) systems will also provide some built-in security

- [ ] reconciliation processes should be carried out by employees independent of those authorising fund movements

- [ ] security control processes used by banks can be incorporated into a company's systems and made part of its own processes

- [ ] segregating payment systems from online facilities is an effective way to prevent random hackers from gaining access to sensitive and confidential financial data

- [ ] IT security systems should be kept up to date, not least to ensure that the terms and conditions of insurance polices are being met. Sometimes it can pay to have systems accredited to ISO or BSO standards

- [ ] external IT auditors should regularly 'stress test' computer systems to make sure they are up to the job

protecting intellectual property

Theft and fraud are not restricted to money. Many companies have highly valuable intellectual property (IP), for example, copyright and trademarked ideas and products, which may need to be protected. These types of intangible assets can be at risk from misuse, and it is an area where the insurance industry finds it difficult to determine triggers for potential claims and the value of the damage:

- [ ] has a competitor caught up with your business by fair means, or have thieves obtained secret or sensitive information?

- [ ] evaluating losses incurred from IP theft is equally challenging: as well as proving a loss has occurred it can be hard to quantify the extent of the loss

If protection is difficult, are there opportunities to turn IP into a competitive advantage? In a number of industry sectors, for example, IT and entertainment, companies have actually made their IP widely available to encourage others to work with their ideas and develop them further. Free or open software is a case in point.

THREAT FROM ORGANISED CRIME

Organised crime is a new challenge for insurers and appears to be on the increase in the UK. Zurich has identified two techniques used whereby gangs particularly target companies in industry sectors that produce and trade in valuable goods.

One tactic is for gang members to obtain jobs on the logistics side of a company's operations or in production areas. These 'sleepers' then work reliably for months – or even years – before they start to ship goods onto the black market. It is hard for companies to identify the source of losses, as the perpetrator is unlikely to be under suspicion.

A second tactic is to target people already working in a company and 'persuade' them to co-operate in the crime. Again, the use of an insider makes it hard to detect the crime early.

However, there are a number of ways to combat the threat posed by organised crime:

- [ ] ensure robust inventory checks and audit processes are conducted regularly
- [ ] new employees need to be vetted very carefully. Specialist agencies conduct adequate follow-up checks on references
- [ ] be aware that employees with personal or financial problems may be easy targets
- [ ] be alert to early signs that fraud is being committed: change in order patterns, inventory discrepancies, increase in stock turnover not reflected in increased sales and profits
- [ ] share information with other companies regularly and try to identify risks early

attack of the clones

Cloning is another pernicious form of fraud, usually inflicted on businesses that deal with valuable goods, such as precious metals, consumer electronics or mobile phones. The scam is simple, but can be devastating. First, the fraudster obtains the letterhead of a company's major customer and orders goods to be sent to a location other than the normal delivery address. When the delivery vehicle arrives it is met by the fraudster, with their own lorry, who explains that the address was incorrect and that they are now responsible for taking the goods to the right destination. Often, they take not only the goods, but also the original bills of lading and the company's driver is sufficiently confused as to forget to remember the fraudster's vehicle details.

A few straightforward measures can help prevent such scams:

- [ ] do not place customer data (business names or addresses) on your website unless you need to

- ☐ check delivery addresses in advance, especially if they are not to the usual location

- ☐ take extra care with large or unusual orders. Set up sign-off procedures, with suitable authority levels, to be completed before the goods are sent on the road

- ☐ establish verification details for large deliveries, where drivers phone the customer before they arrive

The added problem caused by organised crime and cloning-style fraud is that they not only deprive a company of its property, but they can also lead to disputes with its own customers. In a worst case scenario this could lead to contractual penalties and damage to the reputation.

securing the evidence

Once a fraud is discovered, or there is reasonable doubt regarding the honesty of an individual employee or business partner, the evidence leading to those doubts needs to be appropriately secured:

- ☐ preserve evidence and make sure it is not interfered with or destroyed

- ☐ maintain adequate records to prove the providence and integrity of documents

- ☐ ensure accurate documentation about when and where evidence was found

- ☐ consider contracting third party experts to collect evidence

Faced with the risks – and cost – of internal fraud and dishonesty, many businesses realise the benefits of relying on external experts to help them fight this type of crime. Specialist auditors, accountants, insurance brokers and insurers all have useful roles to play in advising business. For example, forensic accountants RSM Robson Rhodes offer an economic crime risk assessment for companies who take part in their economic crime survey. The best form of defence is to be prepared and to know your enemy.

environmental risks are a priority for all

> **Environmental factors are forcing their way up the risk management agenda as a result of physical changes around us, says Stephen Womack**

Directors, their businesses and the rest of society are having to come to terms with new ideas about what it takes to look after our environment. A decade ago, pollution meant the release of toxic gases or liquids, oil spills or contaminating land with dangerous heavy metals. Now, once harmless carbon dioxide is rightly seen as a risk to the environment; a broken photocopier or used phone could be deemed a pollution hazard too.

For example, something as commonplace as scrapping a car, van or lorry is now regulated. The business that owns the vehicle must comply with regulations and collect an appropriate 'Certificate of Destruction' from an 'Authorised Treatment Facility'. The government is still consulting on how to bring into UK law a similar directive on electrical and electronic equipment.

EXECUTIVE SUMMARY

- ☐ environmental legislation is growing rapidly. More businesses and their directors are being prosecuted
- ☐ there are genuine business benefits in managing efficiently waste and energy use
- ☐ shareholders are taking a growing interest in environmental matters
- ☐ climate change may fundamentally alter your business. Do you have a plan?

In England and Wales, the Environment Agency is the lead body on environmental matters. In Scotland the Scottish Environmental Protection Agency (SEPA) is responsible for monitoring companies' behaviour.

In 2004, the latest year for which detailed figures are available, the Environment Agency successfully prosecuted 233 companies – and 20 directors in a personal capacity – for breeches of environmental legislation. Total fines were more than £2.3m. In Scotland, 33 companies were convicted after action from the SEPA.

And businesses will be hearing more from environmental regulators in the future. The Environment Agency's report on its dealings with business says: "We directly regulate only a small proportion of the three million businesses in the UK…our key challenge now is to reach these businesses [we do not regulate] and change environmental behaviour throughout the supply chain.

"We want to see efficient use of resources along this chain and less waste generated. And we want to see businesses making environmentally responsible choices about the businesses with which they work. We will help this process with advice backed up by regulation, including new approaches such as trading schemes. Where necessary we will not hesitate to prosecute."

ONGOING POLLUTION LEADS TO PROSECUTION

Developing computer and video games may seem a world away from the kind of heavy industry traditionally linked with pollution scares.

But Codemasters Software Company, developer of top-selling games such as Toca Race Driver and Brian Lara International Cricket, found in September 2005 how easy it is to end up on the wrong side of an environmental prosecution.

The firm, based in Southam, Warwickshire, was fined £25,000 plus costs of £2,346, for breeching the rules over sewerage being discharged into the River Itchen.

The Environment Agency brought the prosecution under section 85 of the Water Resources Act 1991.

Companies can be given a 'consent to discharge', a legal agreement that sets out standards for the material that can be released into a river. Codemasters had such a consent but had been warned over a three-year period that levels of ammonia were too high.

The firm, which pleaded guilty to two charges, had been working to try and improve its discharges.

It had installed a new treatment plant in 2004 after previous warnings from the Environment Agency. However, two specialist suppliers went bust, which hampered the company's efforts to clean-up and the Environment Agency eventually ran out of patience.

keeping up with the rules

It can be difficult to keep on top of the mass of environmental legislation. The NetRegs website – www.netregs.gov.uk – is a first port of call, providing information targeted at different business sectors, details on existing and new legislation and general management guidance. Companies should ensure that a senior manager or director is tasked to monitor the site on a regular basis.

Changing environmental regulation can also have an impact on companies that work in unrelated areas. For example, higher taxes on landfill and waste disposal, introduced to reduce waste, have led to an increase in fly-tipping. This has led to additional problems for landowners, including businesses. Dumped rubbish can be a health hazard for staff or act as fuel for arsonists and the burden of disposal is passed to the business itself.

challenges breed opportunities

There are positive incentives for companies to manage pollution and emissions risks more efficiently. Reducing the volume of waste produced will cut disposal costs. For example, in 2002 SEPA launched the Business WINS project to give practical help on reducing waste to companies in Northern Scotland. The 17 companies that signed up to the first stage of the pilot are now collectively saving around £2m each year.

The rapid inflation in energy costs over the past 12 months has given directors an extra incentive to revisit energy use and consider strategies for better efficiency.

The Carbon Trust, a not-for-profit company set up by the government, is the lead body on reducing energy use. It gives help and advice on reduction measures and supplies free energy surveys to some businesses with power bills of more than £50,000 a year. The Trust also offers SMEs that meet certain criteria interest-free loans to fund investment in efficiency measures.

emissions trading

Emissions trading started in the UK last year as part of a European-wide initiative to cut business emissions of carbon dioxide, known as the EU ETS.

It is vital that directors are aware of this scheme, because while it initially applies only to a limited number of companies – just over 1,000 in the UK – it will expand to take in more companies in future years.

The scheme works on a 'cap and trade' basis, with companies being set individual mandatory emissions reduction targets. They can either meet these directly by cutting their emissions or indirectly, either by purchasing 'surplus allowances' from other producers or by investing in carbon mitigation projects.

The companies targeted in the first phase are those in the highest energy-use sectors. These include:

☐ power and heat generation

☐ ferrous metals

☐ oil refining

☐ pump and paper

☐ mineral products

The second phase is due to run from 2008 to 2012, with further five-year periods to follow. The government has already indicated it is likely to add more industries to the scheme, including glass, rock wool and gypsum production.

The Carbon Trust has warned that the trading regime will create both winners and losers. It says the winners will be "those companies that take advantage of new sources of income to manage their emissions. The losers will be those companies that do nothing." For more information, visit www.defra.gov.uk/environment/climatechange/trading/eu/

investors are interested too

As chapter 6 explained, assessing environmental risks is now a crucial part of any merger or acquisition. Your shareholders do not want to be left carrying the can for past management failures at a company you have just acquired.

Even if a company's board feels it can shove environmental concerns down the management agenda, the shareholders may have other ideas.

Investors are increasingly concerned about a company's Corporate Social Responsibility – the way in which its activities impact on employees, competitors and the wider community. Over half of the top 250 UK companies now report on their environmental performance as part of their CSR disclosures. And, from April 2006, all stock market-listed companies will be required to disclose in their annual report any important environmental issues that affect their business performance.

Linked to this is Socially Responsible Investment, or SRI – investments made in companies that behave positively with regard to social and environmental issues and that are managing their business in a sustainable fashion.

Morley Fund Management, for example – the investment arm of Norwich Union – now has a team of specialists who advise fund managers on the behaviour and policies of hundreds of listed companies. Their recommendations influence investment decisions across the whole £147bn it manages – not just in a few 'ethical funds'. Morley even publishes an annual matrix, rating the policies of the UK FTSE 100 companies and the top 50 companies in Continental Europe.

Such pressures filter right down the supply chain, with PLCs under increasing pressure to vouch for the behaviour and policies of their suppliers – and their suppliers' suppliers. More companies now require evidence of formal environmental and/or CSR policies as a condition for trading.

Environmental insurance is increasingly being used to transfer or ring-fence corporate pollution liabilities and legacy (historical) liabilities. The London environmental insurance market offers a wide range of policies for manufacturers, developers, contractors and lenders – in short any company or organisation, including their individual directors and officers, who may unknowingly create or take on environmental liability through their business activities.

In the UK such insurance has so far mainly been one-off policies to assist corporate transactions involving potential legacy problems. In the future we are likely to follow the US model where it becomes a more standard annual purchase for businesses involved in environmentally-sensitive industries such as water, waste or mining. More stringent accounting and reporting standards, and more competition in the insurance market are pushing us this way.

climate change

Some of the most fundamental risks to business futures could come from a changing climate.

Average temperatures have risen in the UK over the past decade, with hotter summers and dryer winters. Flooding has already become a more frequent occurrence, mainly caused by a rise in the number of heavy rain storms. Windstorms are becoming more of a threat, lightening strikes are more common in East Anglia and mini-tornadoes are on the increase in the Midlands.

Across the water, the devastation caused by Hurricanes Katrina, Rita and Wilma along the US Gulf Coast last autumn showed how even the world's mightiest economy can be humbled by nature.

Climate change means damage caused by storms and floods in Europe could increase fifteen-fold by 2080, according to one study from the Association of British Insurers (Financial Risks of Climate Change, ABI, June 2005). That represents an increase in annual losses of between $120bn to $150bn each year at today's prices.

Increasingly, insurers are demanding companies take flood risks into account in their business planning. Mitigating flood risk is becoming a priority, from deciding where to site a plant or warehouse in the first place, to having appropriate contingency plans to protect high value plant, equipment and stock. At its simplest, risk management may mean having a rota of staff to call if a flood is threatened who can shift a company's vehicles out of a low-lying car park.

Longer term, directors also have to be alert to the risk that a changing climate can fundamentally alter the nature of the markets they operate in. Take one obvious example – winter sports. Scotland's ski resorts are already trying to develop all-year-round tourist attractions to compensate for fewer days skiing in warmer winters. This in turn has had knock-on effects for suppliers, ski-hire shops, hotels, etc.

Agriculture, energy consumption, retailing, sales of clothing and soft drinks are just a few of the sectors most influenced by weather patterns. Does your business have a plan to adapt to the winds of change?

keeping the ball rolling

Having well-practised business and disaster recovery plans in place indicates to your stakeholders that your business is strong and resilient, says Steve Willis, risk manager at RWE npower/Thames Water and chairman of the Airmic energy sector committee

Barely half of the UK's companies undertake business continuity planning, according to the 2005 Business Continuity Management Survey. Only one third of these are SMEs.

An active imagination can be stress inducing, but it's the first step to building resilience in your business.

It is unlikely that any director asked at the start of 2005 to prepare a list of potential events that could cripple their business would have included: hurricanes in Birmingham, bombings in London, volatile energy costs, the potential for a flu pandemic, the Buncefield fire and a prolonged drought. How many disasters need to occur before the penny drops?

EXECUTIVE SUMMARY

- ☐ continuity planning needs to be driven by the board
- ☐ without crisis or contingency planning, management may be left floundering in the face of a crisis
- ☐ those companies with a business disaster and continuity plan have continued to trade and prosper
- ☐ customers and suppliers want evidence of continuity planning

With the benefit of hindsight it would be a useful exercise to assess what impact any of the above events would have had on your business. The table on the following page outlines what the possible consequences of a disaster could be.

POTENTIAL OUTCOMES OF A DISASTER

The following illustrates how a disaster or unforeseen event can affect different aspects of your business

customers	loss of confidence, markets and/or contracts
employees	loss of resource and business critical information. Health & safety and staff welfare issues
critical supplier and supplies	loss of materials, logistical support. Interruption to the supply chain
premises	loss of access, data and plant & equipment
production/products	loss of capability and capacity. Innovation & development opportunity limited
information and systems	loss of market and competitor information. Potential compliance or regulatory breaches
financing	loss of credit, cash flow and profit
reputation	damage to brand

The list goes on, but if that imagination of yours is working, you will already have identified a number of potentially crippling impacts. Ask yourself how well you and your fellow board members are equipped to respond and ensure business continuity.

Consider the risks covered by this guide. Each chapter addresses a potential threat to your business. Problems in each area have the capacity to 'stop the ball rolling'. How well would your business fare in the face of disaster?

Planning to survive the impact of these risks should be no different from planning the day-to-day commercial activities that form the heart of your business. It should join cash flow, finance and industrial relations as part of the management cocktail directors prepare daily.

recovery rates can vary

Rory F Knight and Deborah J Pretty note in The Impact of Catastrophes on Shareholder Value (Oxford Research Briefings, Templeton College, Oxford)

that companies affected by catastrophic loss fall into two distinct groups – recoverers and non-recoverers.

Some companies see shareholder value dip immediately after a sudden disaster or catastrophe, then see value bounce back and increase beyond the pre-event level. Others never get the bounce back.

Why should some catastrophes lead to an increase in shareholder value? The research concludes that disasters offer management the opportunity to demonstrate their talent in dealing with difficult circumstances. Customers, suppliers and investors rate those companies who win through. The research says:

"The message is clear: catastrophic insurance cover is no protection against the shareholder value effects of catastrophes. This suggests that a company's insurance strategy should not be considered in isolation and should not be viewed as a substitute for high quality risk management and contingency planning systems and procedures."

complacency is the biggest threat

Many companies mistakenly view business continuity management (BCM) as only relevant to large enterprises.

Research by insurer AXA found that almost one in five small to medium-sized companies had been hit by a disaster. One in 12 said it took them more than six months before they were up and running again, while for one in 20 it was more than a year before their business was back on track.

Business success is not only about growth but also resilience. BCM enables a business to understand itself, identify potential weak points and limit the effect of these. The table on the next page contains the outline of the full business continuity process.

Not all risks can be identified and dealt with, but management can be confident that if events occur the business is prepared to deal with the consequences in a controlled and confident manner. A company that has thought about its risks is more likely to avoid them or at least survive them and to protect staff, stakeholders and future business prospects.

HOW TO DRAFT A DISASTER RECOVERY STRATEGY

focus of attention

- ☐ map business priorities onto system priorities
- ☐ people, safety and welfare
- ☐ continuity of critical business activities
- ☐ internal and external communication
- ☐ dialogue with emergency service providers to establish their needs, concerns and requirements
- ☐ establish minimum/maximum recovery timetable

tools

- ☐ emergency plan
- ☐ crisis plan
- ☐ specialist support plans
- ☐ business function plans
- ☐ timetables for recovery
- ☐ task lists – outlining who should do what
- ☐ key stakeholder lists

rehearse roles

- ☐ develop a crisis team
- ☐ identify and train staff
- ☐ test plans
- ☐ debrief after tests and feed lessons back into the plan
- ☐ media training and prepared statements

The commercial benefits are becoming more evident. BCM is a key benchmark within corporate governance and internal and external audits. Today's financial institutions expect to see firm evidence of business continuity management in place that indicates to them that the business is well-run and resilient.

Many businesses now look for their suppliers to adopt PAS 56, The Business Continuity Institute Standard. Clients may require continuity plans to be in place and evidence that they have been tested through dummy exercises

BUNCEFIELD: WHEN THE WORST CAME TRUE

On 11 December, 2005, there was a series of massive explosions and a large fire at the Buncefield oil storage depot, near Hemel Hempstead, in Hertfordshire.

The explosions caused serious damage to numerous neighbouring properties. It also prevented access to nearby premises for days because of the danger of further explosions.

The timing of the incident – in the early hours of a Sunday morning – meant that injuries were light. CBI director-general Sir Digby Jones, said: "It was a miracle that no one was killed, but more than anything it showed that the unexpected can happen at any time."

The Health and Safety Executive special investigation into the accident was still underway at the time this guide was written, but some clear issues had already emerged.

consequences for the neighbours

Waverly, a subsidiary of Scottish & Newcastle, incurred distribution disruption and stock losses at the worst possible time for an alcohol-related business – just before Christmas.

In addition, two companies were compelled to make statements to the stock market regarding their position. The first was ASOS, an online fashion firm, which suspended trading and halted dealing in its shares. It was more than a month before it could start selling again. The second was Northgate Software and Information Services whose offices were seriously damaged. In a statement to the stock market, it said: "The fabric of the building and the fixtures and equipment inside have been badly damaged. The back-up systems are inoperable. Northgate's ability to service its customers has therefore been temporarily affected."

the lessons

Never assume that a worst-case scenario is so unrealistic that it won't happen.

When making risk assessments look beyond the boundaries of your business. Be aware of the risk posed by your neighbours and plan accordingly.

Ensure that if critical systems are outsourced, the provider itself has adequate BCM strategies in place.

before they will do business with you. Increasingly, BCM planning will be seen as a commercial differentiator and unique selling point in the market place.

you are a key element in success

There is only one way to succeed in implementing and embedding business continuity management. It needs total commitment at the very top of the organisation to drive the initiative into the business. Without this, the plans will wither, become redundant and fail to respond when most needed.

Be prepared to commit to:

☐ including BCM as a fixed board agenda item and consider a different risk each meeting

☐ understanding the links and relationships within the business using facilitation techniques to brainstorm

☐ carrying out exercises with staff, customers and suppliers to identify weak links and areas for priority action. Inevitably they will spot risks you have not considered

flexibility is the key for the future

Directors need to develop a 'risk radar' to help steer a course through the uncertainties of the future, says Steve Fowler, chief executive officer at the Institute of Risk Management

Looking to the future, what sort of world do you see? Will disease be eradicated? Will poverty be a thing of the past? Will technology be a force for good? Or, will we live in a world racked by ethnic and religious division, with mankind so dependent on technology that the slightest failure could lead to total collapse of civilisation?

learning from the past

Clearly, our ability to manage the future is improved if we learn from the past.

Would the dotcom boom-and-bust cycle of the late nineties have happened if we had spotted the similarities with the proliferation of railway companies in the nineteenth century, or the rush to buy rare tulips at any price in the 1630s?

Could lessons learnt during the Spanish Flu outbreak of 1918 – which killed 40 million people worldwide – inform our response in the event of an avian flu pandemic?

EXECUTIVE SUMMARY

- ☐ we need to learn from the past and to imagine how that can influence our futures
- ☐ you can miss the bigger picture by trying to 'micro-manage' everyday risks
- ☐ rather than trying to predict and eliminate every risk, you need a mechanism to identify and respond to new risks to your business
- ☐ the Risk Management Standard can help you build the right mechanism

using your imagination

In the words of the commission set up after the 9/11 attacks in the USA, the biggest failure was one of imagination. Despite detailed warnings before the event from the Hart-Rudman Commission that just such an attack was a real probability, officials refused to believe it could actually happen. On a more mundane level is the makers of film cameras who refused to recognise that digital media would, in just a few years, almost completely destroy their industry.

Such failures of imagination are sadly all too common. As children, we learn to ask the questions 'why?', 'what if?' and 'how?' As adults these are equally valuable tools to develop our imaginations.

Reading widely also helps. For every warning of global warming, there is another of the possibility of an ice age. Rather than ignore both, it's helpful to build the bigger picture, to understand the reality that one will be triggered by the other.

It's also important to learn who to listen to, rather than what to listen to. It's an incontrovertible fact that if you've been personally involved in a news story, you will find errors – large or small – in media reports of the event. Why then do we tend to accept every detail we read when we're not directly involved?

Very few articles have appeared describing how the heatwave in the summer of 2003 in Europe turned trees from absorbers of CO_2 into producers of the greenhouse gas. Directors need to develop a risk radar to identify, track and sanity-check the issues likely to impact their business.

trends for the twenty-first century

So what are the risks we should be thinking of? To do justice to this subject requires a book in itself, but the following are some of the key trends:

an ageing population

The ageing population in most Western countries is changing demand patterns for products and services. For example, pensions and the cost of care for the elderly are becoming increasingly important issues.

increased global mobility

Companies and individuals are no longer tied to any one country but can move to wherever represents the best balance between skill and cost. Witness, for instance, the growing dominance of China and relative decline of Japan. A population growth of around 95 per cent is estimated in the urban regions of developing countries while, at the same time, the absolute population of Europe is declining. Such trends will in due course have profound impacts.

the growth of 'interest groups' and communities

These groups – which are often pan-national in nature and facilitated by the internet – are leading to the erosion of the power of nation states and the growth of worldwide terrorism. However, they can also be a force for good, bringing together knowledge sharing, or linking buyers and sellers in areas where previously local approaches were not cost-effective. Electronic 'word of mouth' is becoming a powerful marketing tool.

climate change and environmental impairment

These issues are both often dismissed on the basis that they are so major that no individual business can hope to influence them. Whether one accepts growing evidence or not, windstorm damage and flooding in the UK alone have increased substantially over the past 20 years. In many cases, these have been exacerbated by our own actions, such as modifying our environment by building over floodplains or on sites previously considered too exposed to be habitable.

new risks posed by new technologies

Technological change is a double-edged sword, since new technologies always harbour new risks. The average gaming console today has greater computing power than the best super-computer a decade ago. The advent of 'universal computing' has spurred other changes, both in our attitudes and the social fabric of life.

With technology, the biggest risk is to take too narrow a view and to ignore the wider implications – both for good or bad.

raw material shortages

These are likely to increase as populations grow. Already, parts of Eastern England are officially classified as semi-desert. Such trends have many outcomes: clean drinking water is becoming a more valued resource, which should lead to benefits for water recycling firms and technologies.

public attitudes are changing

With improvements in public health and safety – as well as life expectancy – there is a tendency to expect total security, irrespective of the cost to us all. Legal systems exacerbate this trend, with the emergence of 'compensation cultures' in place of common sense.

complexity

In itself, complexity is a major cause of risk. In simple systems, it is relatively easy to predict outcomes. But as our lives and systems become more complex, so do the risks. Coupled with the speed of innovation and dissemination in today's world, many small individual decisions can quickly add up to a bigger problem.

strategies for survival

A risk-free world is impossible. Safety is found in experience and in learning to live with and exploit the risks around us. The greatest risk is to seek a safe, rather than safer world. By micro-managing risk, we can miss the very opportunities that should be staring us in the face.

Government statistics show that speed bumps cost 500 lives a year because they delay ambulances on their missions. Children are denied the opportunity to learn to socialise through their parents' fear that they may be injured in a playground accident. Balance is everything when considering risk.

There are no simple rules but businesses can help their survival and growth by:

- placing a high premium on sustainability, with attention on side-effects as well as intentions

- building safety nets, through insurance and strong human resource and stakeholder strategies

- ☐ cultivating people networks through the growing availability of universal broadband internet capability
- ☐ using the right 'risk radar' to determine who as well as what to believe
- ☐ conducting scenario analysis linked to strategic planning, thus developing organisational flexibility

preparing for the unexpected

Businesses increasingly need to be flexible to be able to respond favourably to change. As well as horizon scanning, we should develop mechanisms to spot, categorise, analyse and treat risk.

The problem is that most of us are already too busy running to catch up to do this. Risk management – in as far as it exists in many smaller organisations – tends to be a daily 'robbing Peter to pay Paul' scramble of balancing the various activities of:

- ☐ keeping the business and its people safe, healthy and legal
- ☐ securing and protecting the company from natural forces and crime
- ☐ satisfying regulators, government and auditors
- ☐ maintaining product and service quality, and business reputation
- ☐ ensuring reasonable insurance coverage
- ☐ practicing rudimentary business continuity planning

Some businesses will ignore strategic risks until it's too late or only consider them on an ad hoc basis. This form of risk management is largely concerned with minimising loss, rather than maximising opportunities.

a Risk Management Standard

Help is at hand in the form of a Risk Management Standard, published by the three UK risk organisations, AIRMIC, ALARM and IRM. The Standard has been written for the non-specialist and starts with the premise that risk management is everyone's business. It includes simple-to-use tools to systematically identify

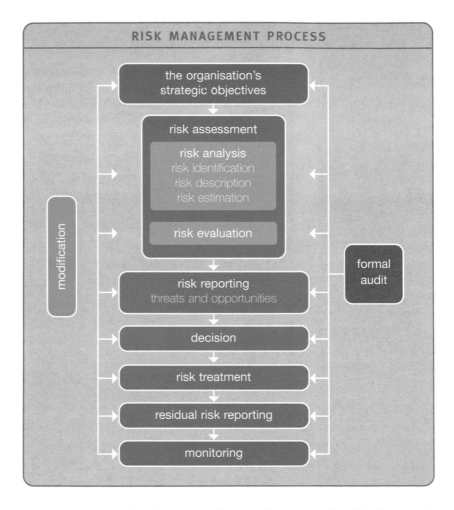

and map risk to your business objectives and then take action. The Standard is available free of charge from any of the publishing organisations' websites.

Also available from IRM is a short guide entitled Emergent Risks, which sets out practical templates for risk analysis and treatment.

Courses are available for directors to learn more about the approach taken in the Standard. These include a two-day classroom based programme for directors from all backgrounds, and, from October 2006, a pan-European multi-lingual internet course aimed specifically at SME leaders.

it's all in the presentation

Insurance plays a vital role in helping businesses contain risk, says David Carlile of HSBC Insurance Brokers

Do you really understand why you buy insurance, what you get for your money and why your business pays the price it does? Understanding how the market works will help you fine tune your risk management strategy and cut your insurance bill.

Directors are compelled to buy some cover by law – employers' liability or third-party motor insurance, for example – or are driven to insure their firm's premises and stock through a justified fear of the financial ruin a disaster could cause. But it may be less clear why other risks are insured. In some instances, insurance may even be taken out as a matter of habit, rather than as the logical outcome of any business-like cost/benefit analysis.

> ### EXECUTIVE SUMMARY
>
> ☐ insurance is only one of a number of solutions to help reduce risk
>
> ☐ a better understanding of how the market works can help you see the broader picture
>
> ☐ work out those risks that you can afford to carry inhouse and those which need to be transferred
>
> ☐ presenting your businesses properly to an insurer will reduce the premiums you pay

Insurance is a part of the management of risk. It is not the solution to all ills and indeed should only be introduced as part of an overall risk management process. The more the risks are identifiably managed, the less amount of 'threat' needs to be transferred. This reduces the threat's likelihood and impact, and thus reduces the cost of insurance.

Prevention is better than cure and if a risk can be mitigated this will always represent a better strategy for any business than having to purchase insurance to cover it.

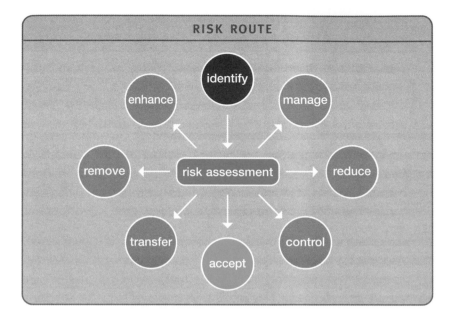

Even when insurance is required, it is important to understand the insurance market and the relationships between the various types of companies involved. These organisations are, after all, integral to the provision of financial protection to your business.

start by finding the problem

When it comes to risk management there is no one-size-fits-all approach, as every business is different. Each risk faced by a business must be identified, understood, profiled and assessed.

The 'Risk route' above diagram summarises much of what has already been discussed in this guide. The starting point for businesses in identifying and managing the risks they face is to assess their appetite for risk. Are you risk averse? What types of risks would you be willing to face? What types would you prefer to remove from the balance sheet? Once these questions have been considered, specific risks must be identified and addressed. Insurance brokers increasingly offer this risk identification, advice and management service. If a business is facing a very specific risk, a broker can also arrange for external specialists to examine their particular requirements. A specialist environmental surveyor in the case of environmental risks is one such example.

Once identified, a risk must be assessed to see the level of threat it poses. What are the odds of something going wrong? How severe are the consequences if it does?

The decision of how to handle the risk will then depend on the type of risk involved. In some cases, risks can be managed and mitigated easily. For example, you may face the risk of a claim from your employees if human resources policies and procedures are not in line with the latest regulations. By simply updating these measures, you manage and reduce this threat.

There may be some risks that a business chooses to accept rather than transfer to a third party. If you run a fleet of vehicles, for example, you may decide that you are prepared to tolerate the possibility of some damage occurring to the vehicles in the course of business and choose not to insure against this.

Losses will occur, probably frequently so. But they are likely to be of low value and could potentially be less costly than any insurance policy designed to cover them.

However, other risks, such as your premises being destroyed in a fire, would probably threaten the future of the business. Although such incidents occur infrequently they are costly. For most businesses, the only way to deal with such a risk is to transfer it. Put simply, you should look to retain and manage high frequency, low financial impact risks, while transferring high financial impact risks.

who do you transfer risks to?

Once you and your broker have identified those risks that you feel you cannot retain, the next step is to consider transferring these risks to someone else. Some may be passed to suppliers, customers or sub-contractors through legal and contractual arrangements. For the majority of small and medium-sized businesses, though, risk transfer would typically involve the purchase of insurance. However, there are other options available.

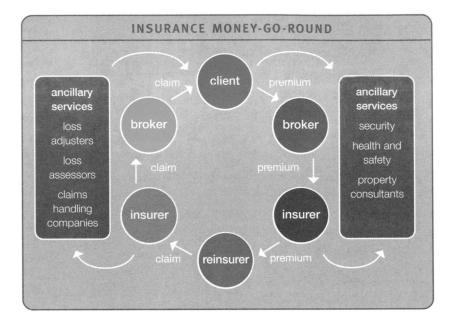

INSURANCE MONEY-GO-ROUND

Some of these involve transferring risk to industry-specific or company-formed insurance captives. These are effectively mini-insurance companies or insurance funds under the control of either a single firm or several firms. The shipping, transport and farming industries have long been users of industry-wide mutual insurance schemes, for example.

Another option is to turn to the capital markets that can offer various financial instruments to mitigate risk. Currency hedging is a simple example, but many more exotic options are now available.

Insurance brokers can help to arrange these types of solutions. However, they are usually only used by large businesses, by companies in industries where the cost of insurance can be quite high – such as the oil and gas industry – or by firms working in sectors where the risks faced are very complicated.

can you transfer your risks?

Not all risks are transferable, as either the insurance markets or other capital providers deem them to be unacceptable.

Over the last few years, some businesses have found insurers unresponsive to requests for financial protection for some liability risks. One example is scaffolding businesses and especially those not actively practising appropriate risk management. This has resulted in such businesses being unable to buy employers' liability insurance.

Another example is the insurance market's well-publicised reaction to companies in the food industry operating out of premises constructed using composite panels. In this case some companies were actually forced out of business because they were unable to afford their extremely high insurance premium charges.

This is where an understanding of the insurance market and what drives it can help you present your risks in a way that underwriters find acceptable.

the money-go-round

The insurance market involves many different types of companies, and in some way, they all have an impact on the price of insurance cover. The Money-go-Round figure on the opposite page illustrates the way in which money moves around the insurance industry.

Premiums flow from the client business to an insurer, via a broker. The insurer then lays off its risk through a reinsurer. In practice, many reinsurers share risks and at times themselves pass on part of their liability to other reinsurers. Claims flow back down the line.

The insurance market is a cyclical one: in the simplest terms, the price of insurance is typically linked to the capacity in the market for a given risk. For example, prices will usually fall if there is a lot of capacity in the market, with both reinsurers and insurers competing for business and chasing business volumes.

This is all well and good while insurers are making profits from their underwriting activities. When those profits diminish – usually due to a surge in claims – the insurance market's appetite for risk dwindles and premiums rise.

Major loss events such as the 9/11 terrorist attacks or Hurricane Katrina also have an impact on the insurance cycle. The cost of motor insurance in the UK in

2006 will rise, in part, because reinsurers have increased their rates to rebuild reserves after the impact of the hurricanes in the US during 2005.

Regardless of whether the cycle is on an up swing or a down swing, it is always possible to present your risk to the insurance market in an appealing light. Businesses that show loyalty to an insurer and employ good risk management practices are best placed to minimise their insurance costs. You may not be able to insulate yourself completely from the effects of the cycle, but you can mitigate the impact.

Insurers do recognise customer loyalty when comparing risks and, even though policies running over three or five years are rare, signing up to longer-term policies can help negate the impact of a 'hard/soft' cycle.

Businesses that can illustrate that they have identified the risks they face – and are managing and controlling them – and that have long-standing relationships with their broker and insurer are less vulnerable to the pricing cycle. As a result, they can benefit from better insurance premiums.

insurance and risk management bodies

Alarm – The National Forum for Risk Management in the Public Sector

ALARM, Ladysmith House, High Street, Sidmouth, Devon EX10 8LN

Ⓣ 01395 519083 Ⓦ www.alarm-uk.com

Association of British Insurers

51 Gresham Street, London EC2V 7HQ

Ⓣ 020 7600 3333 Ⓦ www.abi.org.uk

Association of Insurance and Risk Managers

AIRMIC Secretariat, 6 Lloyd's Avenue, London EC3N 3AX

Ⓣ 020 7480 7610 Ⓦ www.airmic.com

British Insurance Brokers' Association

14 Bevis Marks, London EC3A 7NT

Ⓣ 0870 950 1790 Ⓦ www.biba.org.uk

The Institute of Risk Management

Lloyd's Avenue House, 6 Lloyd's Avenue, London EC3N 3AX

Ⓣ 020 7709 9808 Ⓦ www.theirm.org

Chartered Institute of Loss Adjusters

Peninsular House, 36 Monument Street, London EC3R 8LJ

Ⓣ 0845 3459960 Ⓦ www.cila.co.uk

health and safety

Health and Safety Executive

The UK Health and Safety Commission (HSC) and the Health and Safety Executive (HSE) are responsible for the regulation of almost all the risks to health and safety arising from work activity in Britain. They operate via a network of local offices, helplines, publications and through a comprehensive website:
Ⓦ www.hse.gov.uk

There are a wide variety of advice and information services under the HSE umbrella. The most useful include:

HSE guide Five Steps to Risk Assessment:
Ⓦ www.hse.gov.uk/pubns/indg163.pdf

HSE publication Directors' Responsibilities for Health and Safety:
Ⓦ www.hse.gov. uk/pubns/indg343.pdf

Website www.hsedirect.com has an online archive of all the HSE publications, plus the detailed legislation. This is a commercial site, so access is charged.

Royal Society for the Prevention of Accidents
Works towards accident reduction in all facets of life, including the workplace. A provider of health and safety advice, training and consultancy.
Edgbaston Park, 353 Bristol Road, Edgbaston, Birmingham B5 7ST
Ⓣ 0121 248 2000 Ⓦ www.rospa.co.uk

Chartered Institute of Personnel and Development
151 The Broadway, London SW19 1JQ
Ⓣ 020 8612 6200 Ⓦ www.cipd.co.uk

Association of Occupational Health Nurse Practitioners
PO Box11785, Peterhead AB42 5YG
Ⓣ 0845 225 5937 Ⓦ www.aohnp.co.uk

Other useful resources include:
- ○ EEF stress risk management tool:
  Ⓦ www.eef.org.uk/UK/publications/guidance/public/publication27102004.htm
- ○ EEF guidance Fit for Work: managing sickness absence and rehabilitation:
  Ⓦ www.eef.org.uk/UK/preview/guidance/allmembers/publication30032004.htm
- ○ CBI absence survey: Ⓦ www.cbi.org.uk
- ○ AIRMIC rehabilitation guides: Ⓦ www.airmic.com/rehabilitation-guides.asp

crime prevention

www.crimereduction.gov.uk
Government advice and information site on a wide range of crime reduction issues. It has basic information for all businesses via a 'business crime mini-site'. There is also a Crime Reduction Toolkit for retailers and small businesses.

Business Crime Direct
Regional anti-crime initiative working in Merseyside, but with useful advice for businesses nationwide.

Liverpool Chamber of Commerce & Industry, 1 Old Hall Street, Liverpool L3 9HG
Ⓣ 0151 285 1413 Ⓦ www.businesscrimedirect.org.uk

Arson Prevention Bureau

Joint venture between the Home Office and the Association of British Insurers
to combat Arson. Source of specialist risk management advice.
51 Gresham Street, London EC2V 7HQ
Ⓣ 020 7216 7522 Ⓦ www.arsonpreventionbureau.org.uk

cashflow and credit management

Factors & Discounters Association

Boston House, The Little Green, Richmond, Surrey TW9 1QE
Ⓣ 020 8332 9955 Ⓦ www.factors.org.uk

The Institute of Credit Management

The Water Mill, Station Road, South Luffenham, Leicestershire LE15 8NB
Ⓣ 01780 722900 Ⓦ www.icm.org.uk

Better Payments Practice Campaign

Ⓦ www.payontime.co.uk

Credit Management Research Centre

A wide range of help and advice to improve your credit management
Leeds University Business School, Maurice Keyworth Building, Clarendon
Road, Leeds LS2 9JT
Ⓣ 01133 845750 Ⓦ www.cmrc.co.uk

Chartered Institute of Purchasing & Supply

Easton House, Easton on the Hill, Stamford, Lincolnshire PE9 3NZ
Ⓣ 01780 756777 Ⓦ www.cips.org

environmental issues

The Environment Agency

Covers England and Wales and operates through a network of regional offices.
Enforces environmental and anti-pollution laws and can advise firms. For details

of your local office call 0870 506506 or log onto the website.
Ⓦ www.environment-agency.gov.uk

Scottish Environment Protection Agency
Mirrors the activities of the Environment Agency in Scotland.
Erskine Court, Castle Business Park, Stirling FK9 4TR
Ⓣ 01786 457700 Ⓦ www.sepa.org.uk

NetRegs
This excellent website allows users to examine their business stage by stage,
to check what, if any, environmental rules apply to their operations.
Ⓦ www.netregs.gov.uk

The Carbon Trust
Free helpline number on 0800 085 2005 for energy-saving information and advice.
Ⓦ www.thecarbontrust.co.uk/energy/pages/home.asp

business continuity

Business Continuity Institute
Group promoting good practice in business continuity management and
disaster recovery. Offers free guides and factsheets, sets professional standards
and endorses training programmes.
10 Southview Park, Marsack Street, Caversham RG4 5AF
Ⓣ 0870 603 8783 Ⓦ www.thebci.org

Survive
International body for individuals and companies involved in business continuity
planning. Runs training courses and produces useful literature in this area.
Lloyd's Avenue House, 6 Lloyd's Avenue, London EC3N 3AX
Ⓣ 020 7265 2030 Ⓦ www.survive.com

Continuity Forum
An internet-based group promoting best practice and offering advice on
business continuity. Ⓦ www.continuityforum.org